The Sweeet Old Lady Down the Street
She takes "sw-ee-t to "sw-eee-t!"

Hi! I'm Oberon. Please try to find me in each picture.

Told by Catherine D. Killam
Art by Richard Svensson

Acknowledgments

I wish to thank my beloved husband, Kent, who has supported me in all that I've wanted to do and has been there helping make so many of my dreams come true.

Thank you to Lynn Morrison for her suggestions and her encouragement from the first moment I mentioned writing this book. To my daughter, Kristin, for her encouragement and support. Thank you to my daughter-in-law, Lenae, Marie Stumpf and Ira Ono for their really helpful suggestions. I am also grateful to Joanna Devoe, my YouTube friend, who inspires and motivates me with her upbeat and "can do" attitude.

A big thank you to Richard Svensson whose talent and imagination brought "The Sweeet Old Lady" to life. Thank you to Rebecca Sutton for her generosity and superb editing skills. A big thank you to Koli Cutler for his audio and American Sign Language skills. I feel so lucky to have found the three of you. Thank you to Kay and Carter Sams of SisterPixel for the use of their clip art image of the purple pointy hat. Please visit them at www.etsy.com/shop/SisterPixel.

Thank you to Decy Devere, Norma Beuschel and and Lynn Morrison for their support of Cat-Care. My gratitude also to Boyd Castro, DVM, and his wife, Ann, of Hilo Veterinary Clinic LLC, for their assistance with the cats for all the years.

I would also like to thank my son, Jason, and daughter-in-law, Lenae, for bringing Jayln and Kaylee, my twin granddaughters, into this world. The girls motivated me to want to write a children's book.

Revised Edition September 2014
Text, front and back covers and full page illustrations Copyright © 2013, 2014 by Catherine D. Killam
All Rights Reserved. Published by Enchanted Forest Publishing.
No part of this book may be reproduced, transmitted, or stored in an information retrieval system in any form or by any means, electronic, mechanical, photocopying, recording, or otherwise, without written permission from the copyright owner. For information about permission to reproduce selections from this book, email Enchanted Forest Publishing at enchantedforestpublishing@gmail.com.

For more information about other publications by this author visit www.enchantedforestpublishing.com.

Clip art on text pages purchased from istock.com and clipart.com. They retain their copyright. Purple pointy hat clip art on text page is from SisterPixel and is used with their permission.

Printed in the U.S.A.
Flesch-Kincaid Grade Level 2.1 -2.5

ISBN-10:099107002X
ISBN-13:978-0-9910700-2-2

Dedication:

To Norma Beuschel
I am grateful for her support of
Cat-Care through the years.
I know "kitty loving time"
made a deep impression on her
and she has made a
deep impression on me.

All the author's net proceeds
from the sale of this book are
donated to Cat-Care,
a 501(c)3 nonprofit,
cat rescue and sanctuary
for abandoned kittens and cats.

Please see the last page of this
book for life saving tips
for pets.

*T*here is a sweet old lady
down the street,
the kind of lady you really should meet.
She lives in a red and white
gingerbread house
in an enchanted forest with
her gnome-looking spouse.
The roof is the color of chocolate brown.
It is the cutest house in all of the town.
The moss makes a luxurious
carpet of green
and with the tall trees,
it is a magical scene.

Her face is friendly and full of wrinkles
and her eyes are always full of twinkles.
You know she is exceedingly wise
when you look carefully into her eyes.
She smells of lavender, lilac or rose
from the top of her head
right down to her toes.
Her hair is becoming very gray.
That's fine because she likes it that way.
Sometimes she wears her hair
up in a bun.
Sometimes she wears it down
just for fun.
She's the sweet old lady down the street.

She likes to wear long purple dresses
and threads all sorts of
flowers in her tresses.
She loves going out in funky shoes
and sporting various crazy hairdos.
She has a selection of pointy hats
and beautiful earrings shaped like cats.
She always walks with a dancer's grace
and is never seen without a smile on her face.
This lovely lady is even kind to rats
and she often enjoys dancing with cats.
Her voice is bright and full of glee
and she would never even harm a flea.
She's the sweet old lady down the street.

She gets up early, before the
crack of dawn
and sits outside on the
backyard lawn.
She likes to pray and meditate;
it puts her in a peaceful state.
She listens to the hum
of the bees and the flowers.
Oh, how she loves these morning hours.
She says her secret to a happy life
is not to fill it with anger and strife.
She tries to never ever judge
and to never ever hold a grudge.
She's the sweet old lady down the street.

She wears red sneakers with her
purple jogging suit.
Her cat helps motivate her
with a carrot root.
She eats healthy food and
she loves to exercise.
She knows that good health
is the ultimate prize;
and too many treats will go to her thighs.
After her run,
she'll take a short break,
then make herself a healthy
green protein shake.
She's the sweet old lady down the street.

She has a house just for cats
with special fluffy welcoming mats.
Lots of these cats were
abandoned or strays
who didn't have any food for days.
Some cats were scared and skinny
and came from the dump.
Now they have a home
and they are happy and plump.
Oh, it's so much fun
when she rings the chime
and all the cats run to her for
"kitty loving time."
She's the sweet old lady down the street.

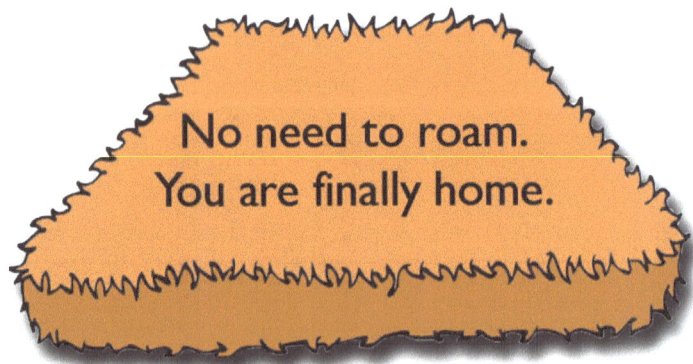

No need to roam.
You are finally home.

She feeds lots of hungry or sad looking dogs
and even takes care of little green frogs.
All her pets have a microchip.
She knows this very important tip.
If one of her micro-chipped pets
became lost, it will help them
get home for a very small cost.
She makes sure they have a collar and tag,
and that really makes their tails wag.
The sweet old lady has fairies in her yard
and she talks poetically, like a bard.
You'll often hear her speak in rhyme,
but just occasionally, not all of the time.
She's the sweet old lady down the street.

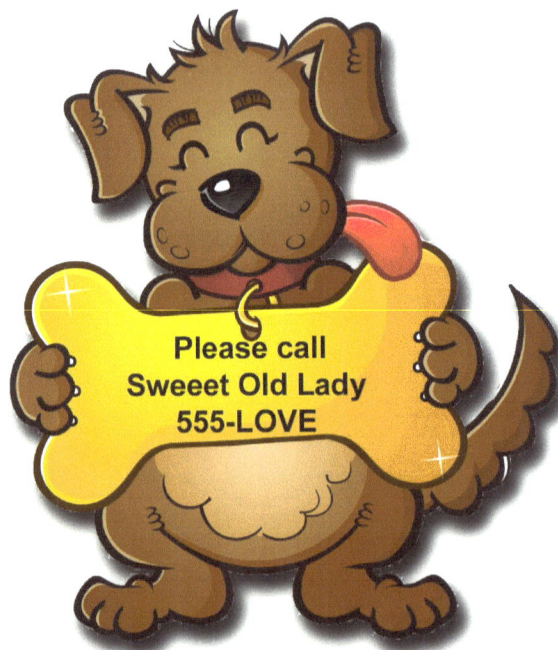

Please call
Sweeet Old Lady
555-LOVE

She has a cupboard
full of enchanting herbs
and she speaks gently
with loving words.
She makes all sorts of tasty dishes
filled with love
and special wishes.
She adds delicious flavors and spice
to make everything delightful and nice.
She has a kind and giving heart
and she makes the very
best strawberry tart.
She's the sweet old lady down the street.

She drinks reviving herbal teas
under a beautiful canopy of trees.
She makes a scrumptious
soup of nettle
outside in a very large copper kettle.
She knows which plants
cure sniffles and ills
so she makes them
into healthy meals.
So if you are one of the hungry or poor
she'll give you some soup
if you come to her door.
She's the sweet old lady down the street.

She must have green thumbs
and magical powers
because her garden is
full of beautiful flowers.
She smells the flowers
after the rain showers.
She says it's a wonderful way
to spend the afternoon hours.
She asks each plant and flower
to tell her of their healing power.
She even talks to the bugs and bees
and you will often see her hug the trees.
Her garden has all the colors of the rainbow
which forms the bridge her animals will follow.
She's the sweet old lady down the street.

She studies the phases
of the moon
to know when to plant
and when to prune.
She loves to dance
to her favorite tune
under the Strawberry Moon, in June.
She'll get so dizzy
she will even swoon.
She loves to watch the stars
float across the sky.
She'll get so deeply moved, she'll even cry.
She's the sweet old lady down the street.

She celebrates the four seasons as they go by.
She even celebrates the fourth of July.
She sings to the stars, sun and moon
a little chant or a pretty tune.
She also honors mother earth
sometimes with reverence,
sometimes with mirth.
She knows the precious gift of each new day
and tries to honor it in every way.
She knows what she does for others
returns to her, times three.
When she says "Goodbye" she always
adds "Blessed Be."
She's the sweet old lady down the street.

Now don't think because
she is old and sweet
that she is either timid or weak.
Oh, no, that would be absolutely wrong.
This old lady is
bold, courageous and strong.
Nobody tells her what to think or to do.
She knows who she is and
to her heart she is true.
If you come to their house on Halloween,
she and her spouse
will give you jelly beans.
She's the sweet old lady down the street.

She has a magical room
filled with crystals and gems,
phenomenal books and feather pens.
She plays with funny-looking cards
and she studies the mysteries of the stars.
She also knows the art
of making a natal chart.
She makes a soothing healing potion of
rose hip oil and lavender lotion.
She also makes a magical ink
and homemade candles
of green and pink.
She's the sweet old lady down the street.

She believes in letting positive energy flow
and she's helped more animals
than we'll ever know.
She's trained in many a healing art
and she gives freely from her pure heart.
She wears a purple bracelet
with a very special charm.
It reminds her,
"Above all else, do no harm."
She firmly believes that angels are real
and they are the ones who help her heal.
She has a gentle and loving touch
and she enjoys helping others so very much.
She's the sweet old lady down the street.

You've met the old lady
who lives down the street
and now you know why
people have nicknamed her
"Sweeet."
You don't have to be old to be sweet.
Anyone can be sweet
and that's really neat!
So if you ever wonder how to respond
when you're in a stew
just ask yourself,
"What would the Sweeet Old Lady do?"
Then you can become a "Sweeetie," too!
She's "The Sweeet Old Lady Down the Street."

The Sweeet Old Lady Down the Street

Score

Catherine D. Killam

"The Sweeet Old Lady Down the Street Song" may be heard and viewed with American Sign Language at The Sweet Old Lady - YouTube, The Sweeet Old Lady Facebook page, and enchantedforestpublishing.com.

2. There's a sweeet old lady down the street.
Down the street.
She's the kind of lady you should meet.
You should meet.
Her voice is full of glee
and she'd never harm a flea
She's the sweeet old lady down the street.
Down the street.

3. There's a sweeet old lady down the street.
Down the street.
She's the kind of lady you should meet.
You should meet.
She wears purple dresses
and flowers in her tresses.
She's the sweeet old lady down the street.
Down the street.

4. There's a sweeet old lady down the street.
Down the street.
She's the kind of lady you should meet.
You should meet.
She wears funky shoes
and crazy hairdos.
She's the sweeet old lady down the street.
Down the street.

5. There's a sweeet old lady down the street.
Down the street.
She's the kind of lady you should meet.
You should meet.
She feeds cats and dogs
and little green frogs.
She's the sweeet old lady down the street.
Down the street.

6. There's a sweeet old lady down the street.
Down the street.
She's the kind of lady you should meet.
You should meet.
She has fairies in her yard
and she talks like a bard.
She's the sweeet old lady down the street.
Down the street.

7. There's a sweeet old lady down the street.
Down the street.
She's the kind of lady you should meet.
You should meet.
She drinks herbal teas
under a canopy of trees.
There's a sweeet old lady down the street.
Down the street.

8. There's a sweeet old lady down the street.
Down the street.
She's the kind of lady you should meet.
You should meet.
She makes a soup of nettle
in a large copper kettle.
There's a sweeet old lady down the street.
Down the street.

9. There's a sweeet old lady down the street.
Down the street.
She's the kind of lady you should meet.
You should meet.
She dances under the moon
to her favorite tune.
She's the sweeet old lady down the street.
Down the street.

10. There's a sweeet old lady down the street.
Down the street.
She's the kind of lady you should meet.
You should meet.
She dances with bats
and wears earrings of cats.
She's the sweeet old lady down the street.
Down the street.

11. There's a sweeet old lady down the street.
Down the street.
She's the kind of lady you should meet.
You should meet.
Her cupboard is full of herbs
and she heals with words.
She's the sweeet old lady down the street.
Down the street.

12. There's a sweeet old lady down the street.
Down the street.
She's the kind of lady you should meet.
You should meet.
She makes tasty dishes
filled with love and special wishes.
She's the sweeet old lady down the street.
Down the street.

Further information about words or phrases used in the book.

Blessed be: The phrase "blessed be" is found in some modern spiritual paths. It's a saying that means that a person wishes another person positive things.

Do no harm: Is a central tenet of the Hippocratic Oath that is taken by physicians. "Harm none, do what thou wilt." is a tenet of some earth-based spiritual paths. It is a concept and guidance for right living.

Funny-looking cards: Refers to Tarot cards which is a set of 78 cards used for meditation, affirmations, insight, and the study of archetypal symbols. It represents the journey of the Fool (the spirit) through life and all the things that are learned and understood along the way, such as challenges faced and ways of overcoming them. It is included in this book to help educate some people who may have negative associations regarding the cards.

Healing arts: The author's definition of some healing arts are: Reiki, Healing Touch, Therapeutic Touch, energy work, massage, acupressure, flower and gem essences, etc.

Lavender: Is a flowering plant. It is grown mainly to make an essential oil which has antiseptic and anti-inflammatory properties. It is also used as a fragrance for bath and food products.

Kitty loving time: Is a special time at the author's cat sanctuary when she calls out to the cats and they come running to her for affection, grooming and treats.

Microchip: It is a chip about the size of a grain of rice that is inserted under the skin on the back of the neck of a dog or cat by a veterinarian. It has a special number that is assigned to the pet's guardian such as their name, address, and phone number. That information is registered with the company from whom the chip was purchased, the pet's veterinarian or the local humane society. The information needs to be updated whenever the pet's guardian moves, changes their phone number or places the pet in another home.

Natal chart: It is a horoscope/astrological chart drawn for the exact time of an individual's birth at a particular place on Earth for the purposes of gaining information about the individual.

Nettle soup: Is a traditional soup prepared from stinging nettles. There are many health benefits associated with the stinging nettle.

Rose hip oil: Is the fruit of the rose plant. It has many benefits to help the skin.

Strawberry moon: Naming full moons dates back to the Native Americans tribes. The tribes kept track of the season by giving distinctive names to each recurring full moon. Strawberries were harvested in June so the full moon that occurs during June was named for the strawberry.

Sweeet: Author's Definition - An older woman who is enchanting, charming, colorful, creative, compassionate, kind, strong, courageous and bold. She embraces and celebrates life to its fullest. She doesn't let anyone tell her what to do. She is true to herself.

Tag: Is a metal label attached to a pet's collar with the name of the pet's guardian and phone number.

Three-fold law or Law of return: Is a tenet held by some spiritual paths that believe that whatever energy a person puts out into the world, be it positive or negative, will be returned to that person three times.

About the Author: Catherine D. Killam, also known as "Cat"

Catherine and her husband live on the Big Island of Hawaii. She and her husband founded Cat-Care, a 501(c)3 nonprofit in 1998. They have rescued well over 500 animals either through reuniting them with their owners or providing temporary or permanent shelter. The residents of "The Cat House" are spayed or neutered and receive veterinary care. The Killams have also prevented thousands of unwanted cats from being born by rescuing cats from their dump and having the cats spayed or neutered.

With the recent addition of twin granddaughters, a new passion was awakened in Catherine. While reading to her granddaughters she noticed a lack of positive role models for older women. It seemed like the only books about older woman had them living in a shoe, having bare cupboards, swallowing a fly, snow, etc., or being cruel to children. After singing, "This old man ..." one too many times, she wanted to sing a song about an old lady. Thus the Sweeet Old Lady was born. It started with a song and ended with this book.

In addition to wanting a book to depict an elderly woman in a positive light, Catherine also wanted to increase awareness on ways to further help animals. She feels that it is important to educate children about responsible pet ownership. In her experience in rescuing animals over the last 14 years, she knows that guardian identification is the single most important thing a pet guardian can do to assist their pets in being returned. A section on life saving tips for pets will be included in all her children's books.

Other books by the Author
"The Sweeet Old Lady Down the Street" Hardback, Paperback and Kindle
"The Sweeet Old Lady Down the Street" Abridged Version, Paperback and Kindle
"The Sweeet Old Lady Coloring and Activity Book" Paperback
"Sweeet Old Lady and The Sweeetooties ABC Book" Paperback and Kindle
"Sweeet Old Lady and The Sweeetooties ABC Coloring Book" Paperback

All of the books are available on Amazon.com. Look for more Sweeetooties books coming soon.
Also coming soon is **"The Sweeet Old Lady Book of Nursery Rhymes"** and **"My Sweet Tutu."**

If you wish to connect with Catherine please visit her Page on Facebook, The Sweeet Old Lady. You may email her at sweeetoldlady@gmail.com. You may also connect with her through Enchanted Forest Publishing at enchantedforestpublishing.com.

About the Illustrator: Richard Svensson

Richard lives in Sweden and pursues a career as an illustrator. His work has been featured on Swedish and Norwegian television, and in a selection of international magazines, books and comics.

Life Saving Tips for your pets.

The most important thing you can do to ensure your pet will be returned to you, should they ever get lost, is to have a collar with a tag and your name and phone number on it. If possible, also write your phone number on your pet's collar. It is not necessary to have your pet's name on the tag. It is your name that is important. Just having a collar is not enough. All a collar means is that your pet does have a home. Thousands of dogs and cats with collars end up at the humane society and, unfortunately, most are not reunited with their owners. Please have your pet spayed or neutered to prevent pet overpopulation which leads to many unwanted animals.

Please make sure your pets are micro-chipped. That is important should they ever lose their collar. Simply having a microchip is not enough either. Kind-hearted people take in animals not knowing they have a microchip. Be sure you have registered the microchip number along with your name and phone number with your local humane society, veterinarian and company who issued the microchip. Remember to update your information should you move, change your phone number or your pet gets a new guardian. A collar and a tag will make it easy for anyone who finds your pet to easily call you and to return your beloved pet to you. Should your pet end up at the humane society, the microchip will help them reunite you and your pet.

It is the author's belief that if all loved pets had indentification, there would be no loved pets euthanized in any shelter, anywhere. Please help make this a realty!

Some food and products that may be dangerous to your pet.

According to the Pet Poison Helpline, The Humane Society of the United States, Doctors Foster and Smith Pet Education, the following foods and products may be dangerous to your pet: alcohol, apricot pits, avocado, caffeine, cherry pits, chocolate, garlic, grapes, hops, macadamia nuts, moldy food, mushrooms, onions, peach pits, raisins, salt, star fruit, yeast dough, xylitol (sugar substitute, used in sugar free gum).

Some other items that may also be dangerous to your pet: anthurium, antifreeze, fertilizers, gasoline, glow sticks, hornets, kerosene, lilies, pesticides, mouse and rat poison, tea tree oil, poinsettia, spiders, toads, vitamins, and windshield wiper fluid.

Please visit their websites for a full list of food and products or consult your veterinarian. www.petpoisonhelpline.com, www.humanesociety.org/animals/resources/.../foods_poisonous_to_pets, www.peteducation.com. Look for foods to Avoid Feeding Your Cat and Foods to Avoid Feeding Your Dog.

There have been many pet food and pet treat recalls. Please check the below listed websites periodically to see if any of your pet's food or treats have been the subject of an alert or recall. http://www.fda.gov/animalVeterinary/safetyhealth/recallswithdrawals/default.htm https://www.avma.org/news/issues/recalls-alerts/pages/pet-food-safety-recalls-alerts.aspx The author is not affiliated with any of the above-listed websites.

www.ingramcontent.com/pod-product-compliance
Lightning Source LLC
Chambersburg PA
CBHW040019050426
42452CB00002B/46